NUMEROLOGY

A Mystical
Magical Guide

*Reveal your true personality and discover your
destiny through the power of numbers*

Hazel Whitaker

BARNES
&NOBLE
BOOKS
NEW YORK

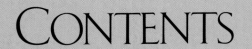

CONTENTS

CONTENTS

INTRODUCTION

Many times when I have just completed someone's numerology chart, I have wished I could have done so while they were still an infant. There are great advantages in knowing which career paths suit you, which numbers in general are compatible with your own, how to interrelate with family and friends by knowing the characteristics of each individual's numbers. It is also a great advantage to know whose numbers are not compatible with your own. If you get the chance, a knowledge of numerology might also help you choose which house you live in. But even if you have no say in this, numerology will help you understand your house number's characteristics. Numerology can give you an understanding of your fellow work mates; and if you are running a business, it will show you which destiny number combinations can work together to give you maximum benefits.

It is sad to meet an adult battling to fit in to a career for which they were never suited. Or to hear a parent complain that one of their little darlings turned into a monster for no obvious reason. Quite often, a quick calculation of the child's destiny numbers as well as their own might well have helped them understand their odd child.

Learning the basics of numerology is both pleasant and advantageous. We may not be able to control which destiny number or name number we're given, but self-analysis is so much easier when we know what we are dealing with.

Calculating your own personal combination of numbers is a simple process, and a step by step guide is available in this book. Once you have learned the basic positive and negative influences of all the numbers, you will quickly advance towards calculating and combining your personal destiny, birthpath, zodiac and name

numbers thus acquiring an insight into your personal characteristics.

You will soon be able to calculate your lucky lottery numbers and numerous other valuable, informative ways to practice numerology on your friends. They will be impressed by your accuracy and you will understand the personalities of those whose numbers you read. You will begin to see where your qualities can best be used, and learn which shortcomings you need to work and improve on. You will be able to forecast the future of the year ahead and the years which follow, thus preparing you for the challenges ahead.

It seems everything has a numerical value. We are governed by the numbers on a clock, dictating time, and the dates on a calendar, guiding us through the year. It is interesting to note "The Happy Hour" in a hotel or club is usually 6 p.m., 6 being a happy number. The "Witching Hour" is 12 midnight, which reduces to 3, a bewitching number. Major events in one's personal life often "coincidentally" happen in threes.

You will learn how to calculate and interpret your own personality box by following the simple diagrams and instructions in this book, and you will quickly learn the meanings of the various zodiac and destiny combinations. The simple instructions contained in this book will provide you with many entertaining hours. Why not have a numerology party with your friends, who will enjoy it and thank you for your unique idea? Keep this book in an easily accessible place, because you will find yourself constantly reaching for it when you are entertaining friends, for people never tire of hearing all about themselves.

MEANINGS OF THE NUMBERS

Number One stands to attention because he is the leader of all the Cosmos.

Number Two sways as he vacillates trying his best to have it both ways.

Number Three knows that he's versatile having a finger in each pie he tries.

Number Four thinks he was born to worry does not want to live life in a hurry.

Number Five simply hates to be bored time wasted is something he cannot afford.

Number Six loves to love and be loved
he's smooth, romantic and velvet-gloved.

Number Seven is intellect at its best
inner searching seems to be his main quest.

Number Eight knows both famine and feast
familiar with both the most and the least.

Number Nine is humanitarian
loathing all things barbarian.

Eleven and Twenty Two won't be reduced
won't separate and can't be diffused.

THE POWER OF ONE

Ruling Planet — *The Sun*
Colors — *Yellow, Orange, Gold*
Gemstones — *Topaz, Amber*

The Power of One attracts the pioneering and inventive forces. It signifies originality, independence and leadership. People with this Destiny Number tend to stand out in the crowd. They want to take over, organize and offer inventive ideas — they want to be in charge. Even though they can become unapproachable, other people lean on them for guidance, depending on the One personality to come up with solutions to their problems.

The karmic lessons which a Number One Destiny attracts are expectations of high achievement; the exploration of new ideas; the rewards of success; and the fear of failure. This destiny requires a competitive spirit and a determined decisive mind. Great physical and mental energy are prerequisites of the Number One character if they are to achieve the success they deserve; but "superior beings" are intimidating, so very often the person with this number finds themselves aloof and alone, bewildered because they love centerstage and thrive on applause. Destiny did not intend a Number One personality to be second best at anything so they choose careers which afford them plenty of scope and control, i.e. scientific researchers, politicians, political advisers, inventors, designers, engineers, explorers, and fire fighters.

At their best, they shine like their ruling planet, the Sun. However, the sun can get in your eyes at times. At their worst, they may become so full of self-importance they could begin to believe they can do no wrong. When this happens, they become tyrants who will not suffer fools easily. They are then intolerant and judgmental.

HEALTH: One people are prone to blood pressure, heart disease and eye problems.

THE TIMID TWO

Ruling Planet — *The Moon*
Colors — *Green, Cream*
Gemstones — *Pearl, Jade, Moonstone*

The timidity of Two comes from the Moon's influence on its duality. People whose Destiny Number is Two prefer to follow and wish to please. They are versatile, sociable, approachable and love conversation, hearing both sides of a story.

The karmic lessons of a Number Two destiny often create frustration because these people are afraid of choice. Many Two destinies follow two career paths; they lack a sense of direction and find it difficult to focus. Fate has decreed they play a support role through life, which they don't mind because they are too self-conscious to lead. Number Two destinies are gentle folk with intuitive and emotional natures. The Moon's influence makes Two people insecure, which causes them to seek the company of friends and partners who are dependable and emotionally secure. Mood swings and emotional fragility can cause despair, often resulting in self-pity. Two people are romantic, sentimental dreamers who require encouragement and reassurance. But Two Destiny people are destined to be the peacemakers of the planet. They do well in the hospitality industry; they are good negotiators and would do well in public relations and sales. They also make good teachers.

Two people make good friends, have a good sense of humor, are good entertainers and good negotiators. Two children are prone to peer group pressure because they like to be popular. Often when there is an abundance of Two's in a personal numerology chart this personality might have some degree of confusion about their sexuality.

HEALTH: Two people are subject to digestive and stomach problems. Quite often they suffer from depression.

THE TRI-MENDOUS THREE

Ruling Planet — *Jupiter*
Color — *Purple, Lilac, Mauve*
Gemstone — *Amethyst*

This multi-talented number attracts creativity, imagination, artistic talents, versatility and good nature. People with this Destiny Number are gifted with these blessings.

The karmic lessons of a Three Destiny Number are designed to teach its owner that hedonistic behavior can be the result of too much luck and too much talent, because their highly creative and entrepreneurial personalities will favor the good lifestyle these lucky people were born to experience. Rarely will this highly energized character be upstaged because they are not only gifted, but competitive. The entertainment industry is brimming over with Number Three destinies and it is not difficult to imagine what chaos results from so many egotists in the one place. Thankfully they are happy people who do not harbor grudges for long. Even as small children people with a Number Three destiny shine, oozing talent and self-confidence. As adults they are sociable giants with witty, amusing personalities. Being unpredictable and charming, they make exciting lovers; but ones who are capable of trading in and trading up when a partner becomes too possessive or boring. Other interesting careers for Three destinies are as musicians, journalists and advertising executives.

At their best, Three people will endeavor to use all their skills to the benefit of all. At worst, they have too many irons in the fire at one time which can make them a Jack of all trades and master of none.

Three people can be highly sensitive and can easily acquire excessive and addictive behavior patterns. They can be lucky, but overgenerous and wasteful. Everything in moderation should be their motto if they are to evolve spiritually.

HEALTH: Three people are subject to skin problems as well as other stress-related illnesses.

FOUR SQUARE AND FAIR

Ruling Planet — *Uranus*
Colors — *Blue, Gray*
Gemstone — *Sapphire*

The positive qualities of Number Four — practicality, stability, dependability and good organization — can make people carrying this Destiny Number the planet's cornerstones of society. They build their lives block by block, but they must be careful not to limit themselves in their efforts to secure a safe environment.

Anyone who crosses the path of a Number Four destiny is richer for the experience because this hard working, faithful personality has a steadying influence on everyone. But rarely does a Number Four reap the credit it deserves. Everything these people gain they have earned through dedication to duty and commitment. Born worriers, even in childhood, they take life seriously and suffer headaches and nervous tension early in life. Four people lack confidence and their greatest need is to be needed. They are always looking for approval but don't often get it — probably because people assume from Four's efficiency they must already know it. As adults they become even more conscientious and dependable, thus making excellent friends, spouses and parents; but they are overprotective and sometimes possessive, causing their children to leave the nest early. Small wonder, therefore, that muscle spasms and neck and head problems seem to plague them in later years.

Four people may have a tendency to be too serious, dull, gloomy or worry too excessively — which could turn them into Mr Plod or Ms Melancholy. This makes them difficult characters for more extroverted personalities to understand. Four people can be blunt and outspoken which frightens the more timid Two and Six personalities.

HEALTH: When Four people are not worrying themselves to death, they are reaching for the headache tablets or receiving heat treatment for a bad neckache. Ulcers are common with this number.

FRIVOLOUS FIVE

Ruling Planet — *Mercury*
Colors — *Gray, White*
Gemstone — *Diamond*

Extroverted, energetic, resourceful, productive, adventurous are some of the qualities credited to Number Five destinies. They are impatient and hungry for the taste of life. People with a Number Five Destiny Number will try anything at least once. They will usually go back for a second serving, even when the adventure is dangerous. Some of the advice I have given people with this number are: "Expect the unexpected", "Go with the flow", but for Pete's sake "Look before you leap". They are very sociable people and love to talk.

Perhaps the reason why so many people with Number Five destinies are highly strung is because their karmic lessons involve them in so many varied life experiences. They are mental and physical contortionists; they are unpredictable characters with an insatiable appetite for life. They become sarcastic and critical under stress and are far too impulsive for their own good, often regretting their fast behavior. They are excitable and exciting to be around and have more casual than lifelong friends. The media attracts many Five destinies and any career which requires good communication skills. They find boredom intolerable because they are active mentally, physically and spiritually.

Their tendencies to be frivolous, argumentative and changeable, and their moody traits can cause Five people strife. Because of their low boredom threshold, Number Five Destiny children should be kept occupied to prevent them becoming hyperactive.

Number Five adults can be found among the sexually overactive community because they can also become bored in the bedroom.

HEALTH: Five people are somewhat accident prone. They can get hurt swinging from the chandeliers or driving too fast. Insomnia is a common problem for Five people and, to a lesser degree, they could suffer from mental disorders.

SENSITIVE SIX

Ruling Planet *— Venus*
Color *— Blue*
Gemstone *— Emerald*

Typically, because of their ruling planet Venus, people of the Six Destiny Number are romantic, peace loving, homely, family orientated, compassionate and considerate creatures who live to love. They are credited with the title "The Beautiful People" because they are attracted to beautiful things and are born romantics.

The homes of Six Destiny people are often filled with arts and crafts of their own creation. They love to potter around, make pots, paint and write. Their imagination and creativity gives them a flair for interior design. And although they are home bodies at heart, they also need to express their enormous creative talents in a suitable career. Musicians, poets, artists, interior designers are among the career choices they should make. They also make good marriage guidance counselors.

The spouse and children of a Six parent are well blessed, because it is within the family environment that Sixes excel. However, when they are in excess of these qualities, they become overly protective of their loved ones. They become perfectionist, which can be difficult living on an imperfect planet, and because of their perfectionist trait Sixes tend to resent constructive criticism. Six people should guard against vanity.

HEALTH: Six people tend to suffer from poor circulation and heart disease. The throat and kidney areas are also weak spots for many Six people.

SOLITARY SEVEN

Ruling Planet *— Neptune*
Color *— Green*
Gemstone *— Moonstone*

Positive traits of the Seven Destiny Number are that they are intellectual, philosophical, imaginative, solitary and psychically gifted. They are attracted to the ocean's vibration and its green/blue colors and they like to live near water. Seven people are very private although not necessarily unapproachable. They are attracted to all things mythical and mystical.

This is a most intense personality, constantly searching for the meaning of life and the hereafter. Intensely sensitive to vibration, which is why they must have a tranquil environment in which to live and work, they are in tune with nature and abhor imitations. They are very psychic beings and the solitude they seek intensifies this ability. Sevens love to explore the religious and spiritual beliefs of foreign cultures, and making a pilgrimage to remote parts of the world is not an uncommon practice with them. Having gathered this knowledge they need to share it with the world, but instead, they prefer to lock their souls away in a quest for privacy and reflection.

Career paths that involve a degree of contemplation would suit most Seven people. They are often found in scientific research, libraries and book shops; they also make good writers and musical composers.

Negative traits of this number are impracticality, secretiveness, inapproachability, moodiness and laziness; as well, Seven people can be very unrealistic. They live in a world of their own and must be careful not to cut themselves off too often from the rest of society.

Children with this Destiny Number should be encouraged to share their gifts with the rest of the world.

HEALTH: Seven people may suffer from nervous disorders and depression. They often have problems with their "water works", their kidneys and related organs.

EXTREMIST EIGHT

Ruling Planet — *Saturn*
Color — *Black, Purple*
Gemstones — *Ruby, Amethyst*

People with this Destiny Number have an appreciation of the material things on the planet, ambition, drive and tenacity. Eight people admire those who are strong-willed and strong-minded. They are outspoken and opinionated, but very loyal. Eight people have feast or famine destinies and all or nothing attitudes. They were born "old souls" which makes them appear to know it all — even in childhood. The old adage: "When they're good they're very, very good and when they're bad they're horrid" fits Eight people. They are people of substance and born organizers. A good environment is essential to them. Eight people rarely try anything until they have made sure they can be good at it. Career paths Eight people generally enjoy include corporate business, the law, merchant banking and accountancy.

Eight people are often satirical about the feast or famine destiny Fate has dealt them, though they should remember they have as many positive experiences as negative ones. They cannot see the logic of a higher intelligence which allows them to work hard towards their goals, shows them the rewards of their efforts, then pulls the rug from under them. Their inner strength seems to be constantly tested, often causing them to wonder how much more they have to prove in order to receive their just rewards. It is difficult for them to understand their karmic lessons because these are not tangible. Once they accept their see-saw existence, they usually find a way to deal with it by storing the positive benefits for a rainy day.

Eight people may have a tendency towards arrogance, obstinacy, extremism and ruthlessness; they may also suffer from depression.

HEALTH: Eight people may suffer skin problems, troubles with their teeth, and rheumatic complaints.

NOTORIOUS NINE

Ruling Planet — *Mars*
Color — *Red*
Gemstone — *Bloodstone*

Cats have nine lives, and humans live in cycles of nine years. People with the Nine Destiny Number are humanitarian creatures who wish to save the world. They are very old souls and therefore psychic. They literally "see red" when injustice is done. They are sensual people, easily attracting the opposite sex with whom they love to flirt, being naturally hot-blooded.

The karmic lessons of a Nine destiny involve the global well-being of humanity. Missionaries and visionaries flock to underdeveloped countries fighting for the spiritual and physical growth of humankind. They want to save the planet and its occupants from self-destruction, sometimes becoming martyrs to the cause. The fighting spirit of the planet Mars' influence on Nine people inspires them to pursue these goals with grit and guts. They are intrigued by the paranormal because they have great insight and innate psychic powers. They crave affection and are passionate lovers. Their super-sensitive natures are easily offended and they do not forgive easily. Careers that attract Nine people are in the medical field, welfare, religious orders, veterinary science, animal welfare, parks and wildlife, environmental organizations and the visual arts. Circus people often have multiple Nines in their numerology charts.

Nine personalities may have a tendency towards possessiveness, neurosis and volatility. God help the person they are fatally attracted to because they won't let them out of their sight for long. Promiscuity can be a problem for them because they are constantly being pursued and they love flattery.

HEALTH: Nine people may suffer problems around the genitals and kidney disease.

ELEVATED ELEVEN &
TREMENDOUS TWENTY TWO

Most numerologists attach a great deal of importance to the Power of 11 and 22, preferring not to reduce them to Number Four or Number Two.

My own observations on this matter have lead me to believe in the Power of 11 and 22, and even though I do reduce them when calculating a numerology chart, I also take the power of each into consideration, because I have found both 11 and 22 often belong to people whose destiny is important and unusual. They have strong psychic ability and appear to be highly evolved spirituality.

Two examples of famous names are:

JESUS
1+5+1+3+1 = 11

ELVIS
5+3+4+9+1 = 22

Both brought powerful, lasting influences to the planet, albeit for very different reasons. Both were relatively short-lived destinies ending tragically.

In some ways these two numbers, 11 and 22, are contradictory. The personality with an Eleven Destiny Number has a karma of independence and leadership as well as the reduced number 1+1 = 2 — that of a dependent follower — to cope with. Interestingly, Jesus was a powerful leader who attracted many followers. Elvis depended on his followers to achieve his fame which he guarded with elaborate security measures — the result of the security conscious influence of the Four (2+2) Destiny Number.

1 is the number of revelation and spiritual insight. The eleventh card of the Tarot's Major Arcana is "Justice". When someone has completed their mission in their search for truth and insight it will be revealed by the appearance of this card in their layout.

22 is the number of completion and perfection. The final card of the Major Arcana is Number 22, "The World", symbol of completion.

WHY YOU SHOULD KNOW YOUR DESTINY, ZODIAC & BIRTHPATH NUMBERS

Many a misunderstood marriage could have been avoided "if only" the once happy couple had understood the best they could have expected from their partner. But it is never too late to learn to understand your loved ones. Marriage guidance counselors would be well equipped to help solve the problems of their unhappy clients if they were fully aware of the more subtle causes of conflict.

Employers would be at an advantage when interviewing a prospective employee "if only" they knew how to assess the applicant's compatibility with their requirements. Perhaps conflict and office politics could then be avoided.

The ability to identify the difference between a "would be if he could be" dreamer, and a genuinely focused achiever is an invaluable skill.

There are differences in the purpose of your Destiny Number, your Zodiac Number and your Birthpath Number — each has positive and negative forces — each has a role to play in aiding you to achieve fulfillment in life.

The information illustrated in the following pages will enable you to understand these forces, according to the art of numerology. To get the full benefit from this knowledge, open a personal file or notebook and record all pertinent details as requested. This way you will build up a numerology chart. For a demonstration of how to lay out and interpret this chart, refer to SOME COMBINATION NUMBER EXAMPLES, pages 70–77.

When referring to the numbers in MEANINGS OF THE NUMBERS on pages 8–29 it is important to bear in mind that the characteristics given for each number may be modified or intensified depending on the other numbers that make up your numerology chart.

How To Calculate Your Destiny Number

Your Destiny Number represents the karmic lessons you will experience during your lifetime. This makes the Destiny Number the most important number in your numerology chart. When you came into the world, the energies represented by the power of this number were activated. Herein lie the forces that determine the potential of your destiny.

Calculating your Destiny Number or that of your children, family and friends, is a simple and speedy exercise if you follow the elementary procedure as demonstrated on this page.

Step 1

Write down the date of your birthday. For example, if you were born on the fifteenth day of June, 1973, i.e. 15/6/1973, you write each number down, then add all the single digits together:

$$1 + 5 + 6 + 1 + 9 + 7 + 3 = 32$$

Reduce these numbers once again:

$$3 + 2 = 5$$

You now know that the personal Destiny Number of a person born on this date is **5**.

When you have discovered your Destiny Number, refer to the positive and negative traits attached to this number detailed in MEANING OF THE NUMBERS on pages 8–29. Write this information in your personal file or notebook.

Your Zodiac Number

 Each of the twelve signs of the zodiac have an important number attached to it which you will find in the graph displayed opposite. The planetary influences as represented by the Zodiac Number have a strong influence on your personality traits. Sometimes these are compatible with your Destiny Number and sometimes they are incompatible — this can make the difference between a smooth passage through life or a rough one.

You may wish to take this number into account when you are searching for lucky lottery numbers, or you may like to assess its compatibility with a present or prospective house number. This number's planetary influence shares equal value with your Destiny Number in these matters.

If your Destiny Number and Zodiac Number are both number 8, say, 8 January, 1961:

Your Destiny Number is $\quad 8 + 1 + 1 + 1 + 9 + 6 + 1 = 26$

Your Capricorn Zodiac Number $\qquad = 8$

As well, this Birthdate Number is also 8. If this were your birth date, then you may well attract money; but this is an excessive combination for any personality to cope with, and a warning might be: "Anything in excess, usually ends up in a mess."

Add your Zodiac Number to your personal file or notebook as the second most important number for your numerology chart.

ZODIAC	PLANETARY INFLUENCE	ZODIAC NUMBER
Aries	Mars	9 (Nine)
Taurus	Venus	6 (Six)
Gemini	Mercury	5 (Five)
Cancer	Moon	2 (Two)
Leo	Sun	1 (One)
Virgo	Mercury	5 (Five)
Libra	Venus	6 (Six)
Scorpio	Mars	9 (Nine)
Sagittarius	Jupiter	3 (Three)
Capricorn	Saturn	8 (Eight)
Aquarius	Uranus	4 (Four)
Pisces	Neptune	7 (Seven)

Your Birthpath Number

Your Birthpath Number represents some of your personality traits. Numerologists debate on the order of importance between the Destiny Number and the Birthpath Number, but for our demonstration we will take the Birthpath Number as being of least importance.

Sometimes you will find that the Destiny Number and Birthpath Number are incompatible, but all character traits, however contradictory, must be taken into account when assessing a personality because there are many complex personalities working out their karma on this planet. Remember, it takes all kinds to make a world.

Your Birthpath Number is the reduced number of the day you were born. For example, if you were born on 15/6/73:

$$1 + 5 \quad = 6$$

Your Birthpath Number would therefore be 6.

Add this number to your numerological chart (for a demonstration, see SOME COMBINATION NUMBER EXAMPLES, pages 70–77).

WHAT IS THE NUMBER OF YOUR NAME?

Numerologists believe the vibrations set off by a particular name can actually affect a behavioral pattern, for better or worse. Calculate the number of your name using the following graph, taking into account: your Christian name; your surname; your nick-name (if any).

Many numerologists believe all names (Christian, middle, maiden and married) should be used to calculate your Name Number, but I would suggest you calculate only those names most often used — these are the ones that are most influential.

1	2	3	4	5	6	7	8	9
A	B	C	D	E	F	G	H	I
J	K	L	M	N	O	P	Q	R
S	T	U	V	W	X	Y	Z	

Example: J O N O T H A N   C I T I Z E N
　　　　　1+6+5+6+1+8+1+5 + 3+9+2+9+8+5+5

　　　　= 33 3+3 = 6 　　　　= 41 4 + 1 = 5 　　　　6 + 5 = 11

Better known as:　　　J O N O
　　　　　　　　　1+6+5+6 = 18 　　　　　　　　　1 + 8 = 9

Personality Traits:　6　　Sensitive, sensual
　　　　　　　　　5　　Adventurous, argumentative
　　　　　　　　　11　　Independence, leadership
　　　　　　　　　9　　Humanitarian, honorable

While taking into account the characteristics of these individual numbers to construct your numerology chart, use only the number derived from the name by which you are best known. In this example, Jonothan Citizen = 11, one of the most powerful numbers. Jono Citizen adds up to 5. Look up 11 and 5 in the chapter MEANINGS OF THE NUMBERS. Because 11 is more powerful than 5, Jonothan would be well advised to forsake "Jono" in favor of his given name.

YOUR DESTINY NUMBER AND NAME NUMBER COMBINED

The planetary influences of your Destiny Number and Name Number combined are significant enough to take into special consideration. Conflicting planetary influences can have a resounding effect on your behavior.

The following combinations are an example of compatible and incompatible Destiny and Name Numbers:

JONOTHAN "JONO" CITIZEN, born on the 15th June, 1996 has the planetary influences of Number 6 (Venus), Number 5 (Mercury), and Number 9 (Mars) brought to him by his name, as well as his Destiny Number 5 (Mercury) to contend with. His birth name, Jonothan Citizen, has the value of 11, which is the most powerful number of all.

Summation:

The *beautiful* influence of Venus may well enhance creativity from the *gifted* Mercury unless the *aggressive* influence of Mars becomes disruptive in this combination, which in this case may well happen, since Jonothan has probably encouraged others to use the shortened version of his name. My advice to Jonothan, therefore, would be to drop the preferred nickname, thus enabling Venus and Mercury to fulfill their duties as positive influences. An added incentive to Jonothan to drop his nick name in favor of his given name is the power of Eleven, a destiny carrying special karmic lessons which must be fulfilled.

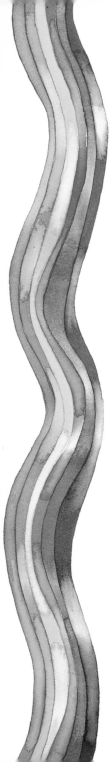

YOUR PERSONAL YEAR NUMBER

The following easy method of calculating your Personal Year Number will give you some idea of what is in store for you in the current year, as well as in the future.

Example: The year $1997 = 1 + 9 + 9 + 7 = 26$ $2 + 6 = 8$

Jonothan Citizen was born on 15/6/1973, but to calculate his Personal Year Number, he should use the day and month of his birth, plus the number of the year 1997 which is 8.

$$1 + 5 + 6 + 8 = 20 \quad 2 + 0 = 2$$

This means his Personal Year Number for 1997 is 2, a year which brings peace, harmony and balance. He may then wish to continue to calculate each coming year in order to predict his future. This way he can tell which years are likely to be beneficial to his goals, and which years will be lucky. Refer to the table opposite for the prevailing influences of each year.

YOUR LUCKY YEAR NUMBER

As everyone knows, some years are luckier and happier than others. It is considered to be a lucky year in numerology when the value of positive and compatible numbers is evident. So, which are your personal lucky years?

In numerology, the world turns in nine year cycles, and when your Destiny Number is the same as the current year number, this is considered to be one of your luckiest years. This blessing, however, occurs only once every nine years, but of course there is more than one lucky year in the cycle. Another fortunate year is when the current year number coincides with your Birthpath Number. Yet another pleasant year is forecast when the current year number and your Zodiac Number are the same.

On the other hand, when your Destiny Number, Birthpath Number, Zodiac Number and Personal Year Number are all the same, then you are in a year of extremes and it becomes truly a "feast or famine" period.

Personal Year Numbers And Their Influences

ONE YEAR	In this beginning of a new 9-year cycle Fate gives you a clean sheet of paper and says write your own script. You are in control of the events in your life and should make the most of new beginnings and fresh adventures.
TWO YEAR	Peace, harmony, balance, communication. This is a year in which you want to develop personal relationships, while many people marry or make commitments.
THREE YEAR	Your creative skills should be used to their full potential in this year. It is a fruitful fertile year and lucky because of Jupiter's influence. A good year to start a family.
FOUR YEAR	Concentrate on building up your resources and personal and family securities. Also favorable for focusing on study and working hard towards a goal.
FIVE YEAR	Expect the unexpected. Travel, change, challenge, new experiences. It's a year of adventure, but flow with the tide, because a Five Year is like a kaleidoscope, forever changing patterns. You need to be energized, alert and ready for the challenges this year will bring.
SIX YEAR	Fate demands you take care of the family in a Six Year. Family matters should be settled, the beauty of family life appreciated. This is a year of romance.
SEVEN YEAR	During this year of introspection you should take the opportunity of examining your inner being and bringing to fruition intellectual pursuits.
EIGHT YEAR	This year attracts conditions which bring financial benefits or losses. It's a time when you feel strongly about your finances, at one time saving every cent then going on a spending spree. People in an Eight Year often seem moody and changeable.
NINE YEAR	This is your emotional spring-cleaning year. Take all your emotional experiences out into the open, bringing back only those things of proven value. Add only positive emotional experiences. Any emotional excess baggage you might have been carrying during the previous eight years must be dealt with and abandoned in preparation for the new beginning of a One Year.

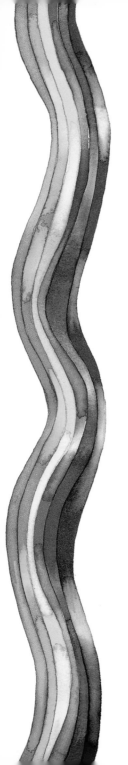

YOUR PERSONALITY BOX

There is another way of interpreting a personality by way of numerology. It is done by creating a "Personality Box" in which you place the numbers of your date of birth in their respective "inner" boxes.

The information you find in the Personality Box has great significance to the understanding you will gain of your own personality traits and those of your children, family and friends.

The following simple step by step examples will demonstrate how this is done. Firstly, you draw an empty box (figure A). Next, you divide the box into nine squares (figure B). Finally, you fill in each box with the numbers one through nine exactly as they are in figure C — the position of these numbers never changes.

Try to remember as quickly as possible just which box each number belongs to. In this way, you will very soon not only be able to view and interpret your own personality, but also that of your friends, thus enabling you to understand other people better, with the further advantage of being credited for your expertise as well as becoming most popular. A rewarding exercise — you must agree.

Figure A　　　　　*Figure B*　　　　　*Figure C*

If two or more numbers appear in a single box the energy of this number is intensified. See MEANINGS OF THE NUMBERS, pages 8–29, and THE INNER BOX MEANING, page 44.

WHERE DO I PLACE MY NUMBERS?

Below are three examples of how to place the numbers of your date of birth in their respective "inner boxes". Refer to page 38, figure C, for guidance.

Example A: Birthday: 6-11-2000

	6	
2		
1 1		

If two or more numbers appear in a single box the energy of this number is intensified. See MEANINGS OF THE NUMBERS, pages 8–29, and THE INNER BOX MEANING, page 44.

Example B: Birthday: 8-8-1985

		9
	5	8 8 8
1		

Example C: Birthday: 25-7-1984

		9
2	5	8
1	4	7

COMPASSION / SENSITIVITY

Figure F illustrates the direction of sensitivity and compassion. People with numbers in the indicated diagonal line show soft-heartedness and kindness when they are moderately positioned (Example A). However, too many numbers in this position will represent a personality who is too eager to please — one who will be easily taken advantage of (Example B).

If two or more numbers appear in a single box the energy of this number is intensified. Depending on the number, the degree of compassion and sensitivity you might have is either modified or strengthened. See MEANINGS OF THE NUMBERS, pages 8–29, and THE INNER BOX MEANING, page 44.

Remember that every number has its own box — it never varies (refer to the diagram on page 38, Example C).

Figure F

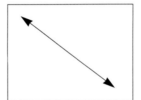

Example A

3	6	9
2	5	
1		7

Birth date 25-3-1976

Example B

³3		9
	5	
1		⁷7

Birth date 5-3-1937

DETERMINATION/ STUBBORNNESS

Figure G

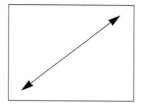

Figure G illustrates the direction of determination and stubbornness. Numbers evenly placed in this direction represent a personality determined to achieve its goals and stubborn in their efforts to do so (Example A). But when the line is overloaded (Example B) you are looking at a personality who will cut off their nose to spite their face in order to get their own way.

Example A

3	6	9
	5	
1		7

Birth date 15-3-1967

Example B

		9
	5 5 5	
1 1		

Birth date 18-5-1955

If two or more numbers appear in a single box the energy of this number is intensified. Depending on the number, the degree of determination or stubbornness you might have is either modified or strengthened. See MEANINGS OF THE NUMBERS, pages 8–29, and THE INNER BOX MEANING, page 44.

43

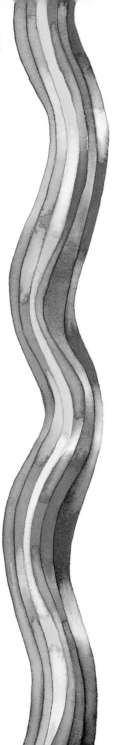

THE INNER BOX MEANING

Each of the "inner boxes" also has a meaning which furthers your skill in interpreting the personality box.

3	6	9
2	5	8
1	4	7

INNER BOX ONE	The growth and expansion of thought, i.e. good communication skills.
INNER BOX TWO	An ability to think things through with an open mind, i.e. unrestricted thinking.
INNER BOX THREE	Multi-talented thinker, i.e. intelligent creative thinking.
INNER BOX FOUR	The ability and willingness to put thoughts into action, i.e. solidifying growth through willpower.
INNER BOX FIVE	The desire to "give it a go" — will try anything once, i.e. adventurous, and sometimes outrageous.
INNER BOX SIX	Loves to live and lives to love. A romantic with high expectations, i.e. marriage, children, family and beauty.
INNER BOX SEVEN	A personality who is willing to overcome a natural tendency for solitude in order to allow high intellectual skills to be recognized, i.e. great potential being credited and rewarded.
INNER BOX EIGHT	This denotes spiritual or religious activity in a persons life, i.e. signifies traditional religious beliefs.
INNER BOX NINE	Intelligent serious thinker with a great capacity for humanitarianism, i.e. the "caretaker" of humanity.

Analyses based on the Personality Box

3		9
	5	8
1$_1$	4	

Example A
Birthday 15-3-1948

This personality displays a determined but compassionate nature. The person is an activist, though not necessarily a leader. They are intelligent, and unaccustomed as they may well be to public speaking because of a slight show of lacking in self confidence, they nevertheless have a flair for it, making them good teachers. This personality also shows a fear of marital commitment, yet has the capacity to fulfill a caring and responsible role in a family environment.

3$_3$		
2$_2$		
1$_1$		

Example B
Birthday 22-1-1933

This personality is a dreamer, always thinking of what marvels they can achieve — if only they had the courage, determination and energy to do so. They are highly creative but lack the drive to activate these skills. They are constantly searching for spiritual guidance, and often talk about what they're going to do. They must learn social skills early in life otherwise they will become introverted with all thought and no action.

3	6$_6$	9$_9$
1		

Example C
Birthday 3-9-1966

Here we have evidence of a personality with an overly active mind. They are usually mentally exhausted because they can't stop the mind ticking over. They become almost super sensitive when someone tries to undermine their intelligence. They worry constantly about the welfare of their spouse and children. At best they are good care takers of the family unit. At worst they are overly protective of same, and may become naggers.

DOES YOUR ZODIAC NUMBER MATCH YOUR DESTINY NUMBER?

An analysis of the combined influences of the Destiny Number and the Zodiac Number can provide valuable insight into a person's personality traits.

Such a system would be invaluable to parents encouraging their children to reach their highest potential. No greater frustration exists than when a parent has spent years educating and guiding a child towards a career which proves to be unsuited to the child's personality. If they had correctly perceived the child's talents, strengths and weaknesses, the result would have been entirely different.

It is both interesting and valuable to observe that Fate in its infinite wisdom repeatedly teams seemingly incompatible Destiny and Zodiac Numbers, i.e. the solitary, intellectual Seven with the extroverted, frivolous Five. Is this Fate's twisted sense of humor or its awareness that it requires us to share our talents with each other if we are to benefit from a lifetime of varied experiences.

It is logical to presume that some Destiny/Zodiac Number combinations have the same meaning, e.g. DESTINY ONE/ZODIAC TWO and DESTINY TWO/ZODIAC ONE. However, there are subtle differences. These come about because the Destiny Number represents the karmic lessons you will encounter in your journey through life, while the Zodiac Number represents the personality traits which will help or hinder this progress. The points listed in the following pages are the main characteristics of these combinations. To draw a fuller picture of the individual personality combinations refer to MEANINGS OF THE NUMBERS, pages 8–29.

The following Destiny/ Zodiac Number combinations can assist you in achieving greater understanding of your child's personality, your partner's and your own. With such understanding, many pitfalls can be avoided, your life's journey becoming a richer, more rewarding experience.

DESTINY ONE/ZODIAC ONE

The personality with this powerful combination is indeed fortunate for there is enormous potential for growth, originality and leadership. The down side is that they could become too self-important, losing sight of the greater good they are capable of achieving.

DESTINY ONE/ZODIAC TWO

Destiny One people are born to be leaders; however, the changeable vibration of the Moon's influence on the usually focused One can make these people followers instead. To overcome this, One/Two personalities need to keep company with strong people who will encourage them to fulfill their destiny as leaders and pioneers.

DESTINY ONE/ZODIAC THREE

This is a lucky combination, One being a natural born hero while Three showers blessings upon it. But if personalities with this multi-talented combination have too many irons in the fire their energy will drain away, robbing them of continuing limelight.

DESTINY ONE/ZODIAC FOUR

The steadfast, hard-working Four influence on the One personality who loves gain without pain makes this a successful combination — these are the people who "make it happen". However, they tend to worry, so may end up with frequent headaches and sometimes ulcers.

DESTINE ONE/ZODIAC FIVE

These personalities need constant challenges and are always looking for new experiences. They are experimenters who sometimes become reckless in their eagerness to "beat the clock". Because they become restless and easily bored, they need to cultivate the art of patience.

DESTINY ONE/ZODIAC SIX

Here is the Megastar with charm, beauty and sensuality. One, the number of ambition, drive and persistence, will bring the creativity of Six to fruition. These people are perfectionists and expect no less from others. However, they need to learn they are living on a planet full of imperfection.

DESTINY ONE/ZODIAC SEVEN

This is an incompatible combination because the highly intelligent and gifted Seven loves privacy while One wants center stage. Perhaps the answer lies in making the effort to allow the influence of the Sun's growth and expansion convince the solitary Seven to share its gifts with others.

DESTINY ONE/ZODIAC EIGHT

The aggressive, serious Saturn influence of Eight combined with the desire for power of One make this a successful, but overpowering combination. Many politicians and other world leaders have this combination. Credited with all that goes right and condemned for all that goes wrong, these people have a karmic destiny which sets them apart from the rest of us, making it sometimes a lonely one.

DESTINY ONE/ZODIAC NINE

This can be an awesome combination. One loves to be loved in all ways while Nine is highly sensual, so there is potential for an overly extroverted behavior pattern to evolve here. Also, an inner struggle may be present because Nine is humanitarian often highly evolved psychically, whereas One often only wants the material benefits in life.

DESTINY TWO/ZODIAC ONE

Timid Two and forceful One can hardly be called compatible, but unlike its counterpart Destiny One/Zodiac Two the Power of One will fight for supremacy in this case. The willing, supportive characteristics of Two are more likely to be acknowledged in the good care of One. The negative aspect of this combination is the tendency to please oneself before others.

DESTINY TWO/ZODIAC TWO

This dreamer too sensitive, too timid and far too eager to please. A follower, this kindest, most gentle of personalities will likely succumb to peer group pressure. Children with this combination should be encouraged to mix with stronger, more focused personalities, thus encouraging them to follow the leader rather than the pack.

DESTINY TWO/ZODIAC THREE
When the vivid imagination of Jupiter's influence is bestowed upon the timid Two personality, great potential can result in disillusion. But if this personality can be encouraged to come down to earth more often they will make good use of the potential for success this combination is meant to enjoy.

DESTINY TWO/ZODIAC FOUR
There is great potential for success in this combination because the hard-working, security-seeking influence of Four is a tremendous asset to the vivid imagination of Two. What more can one ask than to be blessed with creative imagination combined with an industrious, reliable attitude?

DESTINY TWO/ZODIAC FIVE
The likelihood of risk-taking is evident in this combination for we have a careless personality who is too easily bored and only too willing to meet trouble halfway. These people live on their nerves; their impatience and love of speed making them accident prone. Children with this combination should be encouraged to follow their dream in creative sports such as gymnastics.

DESTINY TWO/ZODIAC SIX
Here the Tarot's "The Lovers" comes to mind for these personalities are born romantics. They have great creative talent and believe in following their dreams. Their sensitive, sensual and soft-hearted natures can also be taken advantage of, all too often leaving them broken-hearted — but only until the next time.

DESTINY TWO/ZODIAC SEVEN
Two/Seven people appear to be walking to a different tune to the majority. They like their own space and privacy where they can dream and intellectualize. Though they make great musicians, poets and writers, the timidity of Two and the solitude of Seven make them reluctant to take center stage. These personalities often have an identity crisis and are sometimes confused about their sexuality.

DESTINY TWO/ZODIAC EIGHT

Serious, logical, analytical Eight does not combine well with the dreaming influence of Two, causing inner conflict. At best the peace-making influence of Two will pacify this would-be perfectionist, resulting in a positive and powerful personality. At worst, these people will imagine they are always right and can do no wrong. However, they need to understand there is no such thing as perfection on this planet, for we live to learn.

DESTINY TWO/ZODIAC NINE

Humanitarianism at its best will be the result of this combination. The influence of Two, who wishes to please, is an asset to the influence of Nine, a natural born crusader for human rights. This combination is an asset for people wishing to pursue a career in any humanitarian field.

DESTINY THREE/ZODIAC ONE

Versatile, talented Three combines with inventive One to ensure success for this personality. Children blessed with this combination excel at school and are held in high esteem by their guardians. But such fortunate circumstances cause envy. Fortunately they are good communicators and are able to charm their way out of difficult situations.

DESTINY THREE/ZODIAC TWO

This is a fun-loving combination. While they are fond of gossip, they hold the advantage of having fewer faults than others. These personalities are highly creative and make good writers. Jealous rivals may be relieved to know they have at least one fault — they are tempted to overindulge in everything.

DESTINY THREE/ZODIAC THREE

This combination is the ultimate in creativity. It is full of energy, is extremely versatile and highly intelligent. These people are restless and hyperactive, and can even be frivolous unless their goals are clearly defined. They have a tendency to try to extend themselves too far and, like an overloaded switchboard, are likely to suffer burn-out.

DESTINY THREE/ZODIAC FOUR

This unconventional, anti-authoritarian combination often falls into trouble because of its rebellious nature. These personalities don't want to "fit in". They often find new causes to fight for and can become political. Practical, methodical and patient, these people use their organizational skills to achieve success. Children with this personality combination can become rebels without a true cause to follow.

DESTINY THREE/ZODIAC FIVE

Travel, change and new experiences are constant for this combination. These people are the "Peter Pans" of the universe — forever active, forever young at heart. Many famous people with this combination can be found in aviation, sports and entrepreneurial industries. These people are true candidates for future gold medal performances.

DESTINY THREE/ZODIAC SIX

This is a lucky personality. As our world becomes busier, luck in love seems harder to find. But wherever it exists, these people will find it, their respect and loyalty to family values enriching their lives. Many talented artists have this combination, and regard themselves as being of "the Beautiful People".

DESTINY THREE/ZODIAC SEVEN

Three's joyous Jupiter and the solitary nature of Seven would seem to make strange partners. People find this combination difficult to understand, even for themselves. The highly creative, energized Three, which appears to be so socially confident, is dampened by Seven's need for tranquillity. But in order to achieve success, this odd couple must learn to tolerate the differences in their needs.

DESTINY THREE/ZODIAC EIGHT

The cynical, analytical Eight influence on multi-talented Three has potential for success in several directions. Eight personalities want a written guarantee of success before exerting too much energy; Three knows it can win by virtue of its energy and creativity. These numbers combined have all the ingredients needed for success.

DESTINY THREE/ZODIAC NINE

This intuitive, sympathetic combination is quite compatible. Nine never stops in its quest to do good for humanity, and Three provides the energy and creativity necessary for these undertakings. The Nine personality does not understand the injustice when bad things happen. Fortunately Three's sense of humor lightens the impact of negative actions.

DESTINY FOUR/ZODIAC ONE

The Builder (Four) having met the Inventor (One) can create for the owner of this personality combination a rock solid future. The innate stubbornness of Four, however, will sometimes restrict the speed of growth inevitable to One. Either way, sooner or later, this forceful combination will commit to the task at hand.

DESTINY FOUR/ZODIAC TWO

We can only presume life was not meant to be easy for this combination because the influence of Four's insistence on commitment versus Two's panic at the very idea can hardly be labeled compatible, which is why people with this combination seem to change their minds and moods as often as they change clothes.

DESTINY FOUR/ZODIAC THREE

Jupiter needs to convince the sceptical Four personality that its favors are well intended and permanent. Four people don't like to leave things to chance; they are hard-working, honest plodders. Fortunately for them, however, Jupiter's beneficial influence on the Three personality will persist in bestowing good fortune on the Four Destiny.

DESTINY FOUR/ZODIAC FOUR

This serious-minded combination is reliable, trustworthy, honorable and diligent, but they are worriers and confrontational. They will lay down their lives for their loved ones and expect nothing less in return. Parents with children of this personality combination should encourage them to mix with more extroverted personalities, thus encouraging them to take themselves less seriously.

DESTINY FOUR/ZODIAC FIVE

These opposites need each other. Four is too fervent and Five is too frivolous; left to their own devices, here is a recipe for disaster. However, when Fate matches these two forces, an interesting, talented individual seems to evolve, transforming this combination into a lovable personality.

DESTINY FOUR/ZODIAC SIX

These confident personalities ooze beauty, grace and charm. Attracted to the arts, their names can often be found in the credits of movies. No guardian of a child with this combination should reprimand them for dreaming of stardom. It's better to encourage them to fulfill their dreams, for they will find a way to achieve their goals with or without support.

DESTINY FOUR/ZODIAC SEVEN

Many musical and literary giants have this combination. The philosophical, solitary Seven does not object to the serious, hard-working Four, so when they are combined, everyone else becomes the beneficiaries of their talents and dedication. These personalities are content to busy themselves in a world of their own.

DESTINY FOUR/ZODIAC EIGHT

This fearless combination is difficult to ignore being strong-willed and strong-minded. Often labeled "the salt of the earth", what you see is what you get with these people. They are critical, analytical, logical and honest. Their strength intimidates most other combinations, which is rather sad because they make the most loyal partners and friends.

DESTINY FOUR/ZODIAC NINE

Though this combination of the solid, down to earth Four and the mystical, magical Nine appears incompatible, they are not, because earthy Four needs the compassion which Nine provides. This combination attracts the emotionally weak — hence they have a reputation for poor choices in relationships. These people are too sensitive, too emotional and far too easily hurt, so they frustrate others. When abandoned, the Four/Nine personality is capable of great vengeance.

DESTINY FIVE/ZODIAC ONE

The pioneering spirit of One compliments the adventurous spirit of Five in this combination. New experiences are embraced and challenge becomes a key word. Attractive people, they exude self-confidence and make friends easily. Thirsty for knowledge and thirsty for life, the spiritual karma of these people takes them far and wide. Their negative aspects are restlessness and boredom; these excitable characters tend to flirt with danger and are extremely impatient.

DESTINY FIVE/ZODIAC TWO

This captivating combination loves an audience. They are versatile, adaptable and, like the chameleon, fit into any background. Their talent for the theatrical makes them popular. The danger this combination presents is that their tendency to want to please all the people all the time, along with their fragility, can cause these people to become fickle-minded "loose canons".

DESTINY FIVE/ZODIAC THREE

Outrageous behavior is no stranger to this extroverted combination. These personalities have a great sense of humor and make good comedians. Attention-getters who can steal the limelight without effort, this combination invites competition and challenge. They are also thrill-seeking globe-trotters fascinated by cultural differences.

DESTINY FIVE/ZODIAC FOUR

Thrill-seeking Five and cautious, conservative Four make an incompatible combination. How then do they manage to share the same personality? Here are two opposing personalities sharing one destiny, gathering experience from very different sources. But they invariably succeed in accomplishing their goals and their interesting, difficult karma.

DESTINY FIVE/ZODIAC FIVE

These people are emotional and physical contortionists. Excessive behavior patterns are common among these extroverted, multi-talented personalities. Impulsive and impatient, these people should be encouraged to burn up some of the energy and competitive spirit in the pursuit of sport. Many famous athletes have this combination.

DESTINY FIVE/ZODIAC SIX

A combination loaded with talent and blessed with a good personality. The creative arts are full of people with this combination. Their entrepreneurial skills are evident from an early age. Witty and agreeable, these people are very popular. Under negative influences, however, they become indolent, extravagant and fickle. Fortunately, they only have to turn the charm back on and they are easily forgiven.

DESTINY FIVE/ZODIAC SEVEN

This is a chaotic combination where the solitary, mysterious, sensitive Seven fails to inspire the fidgety Five to sort out its priorities. Five is daring and loves challenge; Seven is quiet, serene and intellectual, so inner turmoil often is the result of this combination. Yet they must learn to tolerate each other so these people need discipline from an early age if they are to benefit from the many positive influences in this combination.

DESTINY FIVE/ZODIAC EIGHT

The well-disciplined influence of Eight on the sometimes unruly Five is good value, but too often logic robs this combination of sensitivity. These two industrious, self-motivated numbers make a good business combination, but must learn to relax — yoga is good exercise for them. The negative aspect of people with this combination is their inclination to lack tolerance.

DESTINY FIVE/ZODIAC NINE

This dynamic combination is determined and relentless in their pursuit of good or evil. These people have more manipulative skills than any other number combination. They will use these skills to have the enemy eating out of the palms of their hands — "Welcome to my parlour, said the spider to the fly".

DESTINY SIX/ZODIAC ONE

Six aligned with One is a combination of intelligence and expansion. No mountain is too high, no goal unachievable. Beauty, brains and ambition are a rarity when combined, so these people are blessed. The influence of the romantic Six on the original One is creative, and most appealing to the opposite sex. This is also an affectionate, extroverted combination which, if abused, can become promiscuous.

DESTINY SIX/ZODIAC TWO

Romantic, dreamy personalities evolve from this combination. These gentle folk are easy going, laid back and imaginative. But they are easily manipulated and too easily influenced. They dislike confrontation and, in a well-intentioned effort to please, will tell you what they think you want to hear rather than what they really feel. An easy to take, pleasant personality nonetheless.

DESTINY SIX/ZODIAC THREE

This combination is versatile, creative and generous. These personalities also have great imaginations. As hosts they will spare no expense in pleasing their guests, but as guests, they will indulge themselves. They love compliments, thrive on praise, and will give due credit in return. They are sociable beings who are ever young at heart.

DESTINY SIX/ZODIAC FOUR

Six personalities are loving and giving; Fours can be found working hard for a living — together they are sensitive and reliable, making this combination a wonderful twosome. The world would be a better place if we had more of these personalities in it. Their super-sensitivity is perhaps their only downfall — they are always ready to go back into their shells, thus depriving us of their valuable contribution.

DESTINY SIX/ZODIAC FIVE

The creative, sensual Six influence combined with the acrobatic Five makes this a potentially winning combination. However, this combination is afraid of losing. These people foolishly tell themselves: "If I don't expect to win, then just maybe I will — or at least I won't be disappointed if I don't." This doesn't make a lot of sense because they are creating negative conditions, putting them at a disadvantage.

DESTINY SIX/ZODIAC SIX

This beautiful, romantic combination has a commitment to traditional family values which would seem enviable, except when their devotion to children and spouse is taken to the extreme, making them possessive and overprotective. The welfare of others is a priority to them, unless they become interfering and smothering. Seldom do these personalities seek reward — a simple pat on the back and a show of appreciation will inspire them to continue their dedication to the benefit of humankind.

DESTINY SIX/ZODIAC SEVEN

The influence of Neptune which covers dreams and fantasies will have a resounding effect on Six's love of beauty and harmony, making this a compatible combination. However, these qualities are easily bruised if verbal abuse is inflicted upon these people, who try to avoid confrontation — they prefer to think we live in a perfect world.

DESTINY SIX/ZODIAC EIGHT

Sensitive Six personalities often find themselves in emotional torment when faced with the intolerant, critical Eight influence. Eight personalities are moralistic with a strong code of ethics, whereas Six personalities exude spontaneity, making this combination difficult and incompatible. To counter the restricting influence of extremist Eight on the natural grace and charm of Six, these people would be well advised to focus more on their innate Six qualities.

DESTINY SIX/ZODIAC NINE

This combination lives to love. They are highly creative individuals who love the arts, nature, and humanity. In love, they prefer to chase and conquer. Good moral examples in youth can make the difference between this combination becoming sexually appealing, or brutal and aggressive with an insatiable sex drive.

DESTINY SEVEN/ZODIAC ONE

The organizational abilities of One are strong enough to persuade dreamy, elusive Seven to become focused and methodical, making this combination ambitious and confident in the pursuit of excellence. These personalities have a thirst for spiritual knowledge, and the leadership talent of One encourages mystical Seven to extend itself in order to achieve spiritual growth. Real and imaginary health problems are common in these personalities, making them constant visitors to the doctor and pharmacy.

DESTINY SEVEN/ZODIAC TWO

Illusion and imagination are strong in this combination, making these personalities good magicians. Seven and Two are compatible because they both spend more time in fantasyland than the real world. Seven/Two people have intelligent and creative minds often becoming artists, poets and novelists. Like the Two/Seven combination, they have delicate constitutions and imaginary health problems.

DESTINY SEVEN/ZODIAC THREE

Great expectations lead to greater achievements, or so this combination believes, and why not? With the intellect of the Seven influence and the many talents of Three, they are advantaged from the beginning. Combine these gifts with their strong religious/spiritual beliefs, these people have every right to believe the gods are on their side. Their only real headache is deciding which career they should dedicate themselves to. They may make the mistake of trying to do too many things — this will lead to poor quality and lack of energy.

DESTINY SEVEN/ZODIAC FOUR

The philosophical influence of Seven on the practical Four makes this combination a compatible duo. As well as the enormous effort and energy these people readily put into their goals, they are often surprised to find themselves in the right place at the right time, just when they thought their efforts were futile. The security-conscious Four needs material reward for effort — the serious Seven needs intellectual recognition. A tall order indeed, but one which Fate seems pleased to give them.

DESTINY SEVEN/ZODIAC FIVE

Philosophical Seven combined with the active, yet impatient, influence of Five has people with this combination globe-trotting, either mentally or physically, for spiritual answers to the secret of life. They spend hours theorizing about karma — theirs and everyone else's. "Why?" is their favorite word. Many people with this odd combination are mathematicians, musicians and teachers.

DESTINY SEVEN/ZODIAC SIX

Spontaneous Six meets solitary Seven in this combination yet these personalities can be most compatible, perhaps because of their mutual love of beauty, art, literature and music. They love animals, and are able to see the beauty in all nature. Often they allow their intuition to develop into psychic ability. When life is not "sweet", they have a tendency to indulge in other "sweets", overcompensating for being sad or lonely.

DESTINY SEVEN/ZODIAC SEVEN

Double Sevens are often psychically aware from an early age, so these people are attracted to all aspects of the occult — impressed by its good influences and compelled to investigate its dark side. Children under this influence are in great need of spiritual guidance, to learn the difference between good and evil as soon as possible, or they will use these powers to escape reality. They are "old souls" whose spiritual growth should not be stinted by narrow-minded, short-sighted guardians.

DESTINY SEVEN/ZODIAC EIGHT

Eight knows exactly what it wants and how to get it, even if the road to success is hard and long. Seven is more inclined to review the situation over and over again if necessary. Eight is methodical, precise and hard-working, making every post a winner. Seven is not governed by the clock or calendar — for them, it matters not when, where, or how but only if. Inner conflict can be a result of this odd combination, causing mood changes.

DESTINY SEVEN/ZODIAC NINE

Creative, artistic, psychic, humanitarian — all of these qualities are housed in this combination. These people prefer to work alone, behind the scenes. They are serious people who become totally absorbed in their quest. Seven/Nine people tend to be emotionally insecure as a result of neglecting their social skills. They have a reputation for being unlucky in love, because they often choose partners whom they consider worthy of "saving", but who may not wish to be "saved". They also have an uncanny knack for being attracted to those of the opposite sex who are not attracted to them. They have much to offer in relationships, they just need to learn the best types for them.

DESTINY EIGHT/ZODIAC ONE

Never say never and never give in to your weaknesses — so say these personalities for they are determined, focused and dedicated. If at first you don't succeed, then change your tactics, but don't stop trying. Though prone to fits of depression when their efforts are thwarted, they bounce back again and again. In many ways these people tread a lonely path, because others find them difficult to understand. They are objective and fair-minded; ambitious but deserving of reward; pioneering but willing to share new ground.

DESTINY EIGHT/ZODIAC TWO

This combination produces personalities of a cautious and suspicious nature. The logical influence of Eight on the passive Two can make these people difficult for others to understand. The confrontational aspect of Eight on the timid Two will create a sense of imbalance at times in this personality, causing them sometimes to be insecure. They have a satirical sense of humor; but when feeling insecure will try to disguise it by being sarcastic, and this does them no good at all.

DESTINY EIGHT/ZODIAC THREE

The energetic, versatile and very creative influence of Three on the hard-working, staid Eight personality does wonders for this combination. Though they are an odd couple, they need each other to create a balance. The pessimistic Eight may govern the optimistic Three in this duo but welcomes it nevertheless, sometimes even allowing the creativity of Three to work its magic on the more practical talents of Eight.

DESTINY EIGHT/ZODIAC FOUR

This winning combination is capable, reliable but sometimes overly cautious. These people will achieve great things because of their dedication to hard work. Honest and tenacious, they have strong organizational qualities. These very serious-minded personalities are sometimes afraid that others may find them boring, but they have much to offer the world.

DESTINY EIGHT/ZODIAC FIVE

Both these numbers love challenge and new experiences. However, this is where their similarities end. The responsible, respectable influence of Eight seems incompatible with the restless, risk-taking Five. It is a difficult personality combination to cope with, but these people should remember that the Five brings a sense of humor and adventure to the otherwise stoic, steadfast Eight.

DESTINY EIGHT/ZODIAC SIX

This is perhaps the "catch of the day" if one is looking for a partner in life, for what better qualities can one wish for than the combination of a loyal, trustworthy, dedicated, love and caring nature such as this? This Eight/Six personality makes wonderful partners and parents for they will make a career of their marriage and parenting.

DESTINY EIGHT/ZODIAC SEVEN

Wanting and getting the best of all worlds seems to be the lifetime mission of people with this personality combination — a quest in which they are unstoppable. They are wise and persevering in the face of adversity, and you should never underestimate the capabilities of this twosome because when this character reaches for the sky, the angels will likely move heaven to indulge them.

DESTINY EIGHT/ZODIAC EIGHT

This combination is in excess. These personalities must learn to tolerate a destiny which is too serious, too analytical, too practical and too restrictive. They are wise beyond their years, almost from the cradle. They are extremely outspoken and opinionated. Their special organizational skills are well known to their friends who, in an off-beat way, salute this ability by allowing them to take over their problems and reorganize their lives. Eight/Eight people are tenacious, leaving nothing to chance. They are self-disciplined and focused; determined, stubborn and strong-willed. They are dependable and loyal, making them good partners and best friends. They have extreme attitudes and their luck is a roller coaster ride of feast or famine. Men are intimidated by female double Eights who can bruise their male egos with their no-nonsense attitudes. If under misguided influences, people in authority with this combination could become power hungry and sometimes abusive.

DESTINY EIGHT/ZODIAC NINE

When you combine humanitarianism with commonsense, the result is a responsible, caring personality who is able to assume a position of authority without becoming drunk with power. These personalities are courageous and compassionate. One of their problems is that they often take themselves too seriously, lacking a sense of humor, something which would enhance this otherwise great personality. Nevertheless, we could use more world leaders with this combination because of their innate power to restructure a seriously damaged universe. They are ambitious, stoic, dependable characters who wish to be of service to others.

DESTINY NINE/ZODIAC ONE

These self-propelled personalities owe their competitive spirits to the Mars/Sun influence. They are indestructible in triumph, but can be poor losers. They will spare no expense in achieving their goals. Business or marriage partners who share this combination will find themselves in a constant power struggle.

DESTINY NINE/ZODIAC TWO

Personalities with this combination are good negotiators. The Nine/Two characteristics are an asset to careers such as marriage guidance counselors and welfare workers. Fate seems to compel them to seek employment in humanitarian fields where they do their best work. Neptune's waters have a calming effect on the fiery Mars influence, but these characters can become disillusioned when they do not know their boundaries. Here is a combination of mixed emotions and super sensitivity.

DESTINY NINE/ZODIAC THREE

What great balls of energy are the personalities with this combination. They only ever seem to stop in order to recharge their batteries, then off they go again. They are blessed with a good sense of humor and great wit. This is a lucky, multi-talented combination. Gift ideas for these happy, vain creatures would be: a new mirror because their last one will be well worn; the latest CD to dance to; and some trendy clothes to show off with. They will not grow old graciously and they love to tease the opposite sex. Impulsive and impatient, to them everything is a game.

DESTINY NINE/ZODIAC FOUR

This combination is likely to have a short fuse. Nine/Four people are easily agitated, causing some erratic behavior patterns to evolve. Fate seems determined to keep them waiting, making sure they earn their stripes in career and love matters. Fortunately, they are workaholics who are too busy to watch the clock. Any success they get, they have earned, so they don't look for favors. Fame and fortune don't come easily to these personalities, but they certainly deserve it.

DESTINY NINE/ZODIAC FIVE

Highly creative and energized, these personalities love challenge, change and new experiences. They are quick to learn and quick to criticize. Lovers of debate, they sometimes stir up trouble just for the sake of a good argument. Though they are humanitarian by nature, they can be intolerant of people less intelligent than themselves. They need to be needed, but should avoid emotionally feeble people. These personalities have excellent persuasive talents and can charm their way out of trouble when cornered. They are even good at forgery and fraud. Destiny Nine/Zodiac Six people are sensual beings who can sometimes become quite outrageous.

DESTINY NINE/ZODIAC SIX

Beauty, harmony, tranquillity describe this combination. These personalities will do anything to achieve these qualities in their lives. But their eagerness often compels them to take short cuts. They collect many lovers during a lifetime because the opposite sex finds them so attractive. They have good imaginations and are very creative.

DESTINY NINE/ZODIAC SEVEN

This personality combination is inspired and highly psychic. These people believe their mission in life is to find the secret of the afterlife. And being more in touch with the spirit life than the earthly one, they often forget they are on a material planet. They have little or no regard for materialism, causing them to mismanage their financial and material commitments. They muddle through life and are unrealistic in their hopes and dreams.

DESTINY NINE/ZODIAC EIGHT

People with this stubborn and determined combination will stop at nothing to achieve their goals. They are focused, diligent personalities who will work tirelessly for what they consider worthwhile. If thwarted in their efforts, they can make dangerous enemies, so it is important these personalities learn compassion and forgiveness early in life.

DESTINY NINE/ZODIAC NINE

This forceful, fiery combination produces personalities with character and courage. These people prefer to make their own rules and regulations, then follow them with gusto. They are confrontational when fighting other people's battles, but will probably seek sympathy when their pride is wounded. Self-sacrificing, Nine/Nine people can become martyrs when fighting for a cause. They are dedicated and efficient workers whose drive is vocational rather than career-driven. On the lighter side of life, Nine/Nine people ooze sex appeal, and enjoy to the full the attention they receive.

Does Your Destiny Number Complement Your House Number?

It is not always possible to choose the number of the house we live in. However, it is beneficial to know what to expect from the combination of the personal numbers of the people living in the house and your house number.

Houses often attract epithets, e.g. crazy house — noisy house — peaceful house — spooky house — warm house — cold house — these can be attributed to the potency of the numerical value of a house number combined with the personal numbers of the occupants.

Some numerologists believe in using the Fadic System to calculate the house number value, and others believe that all the numbers of the house should be taken into consideration. The Fadic system is the simple method of reducing numbers, i.e. apartment 20 at number 231 Smith Street would be 20/231 Smith Street = 2+0+2+3+1 = 8. Therefore the value of 8 only is taken into consideration.

Numerologists who believe in assessing the value of all these numbers would take the importance of a double 2, and the 3 and 1 into consideration. So-called "houses of evil" are often the result of a negative combination of numbers just as "houses of harmony" are the result of a positive combination of numbers. Too many components of the same number is best avoided if possible because it stunts spiritual growth and is too extreme. A house number 44, with more than one 4 personality living there, would most likely have bars on the window and a top security alarm system — 4 is a security-conscious number which creates nervous tension. A house with too many 5s (an extroverted and liberated number) can quickly gain a reputation for being too loud.

The following pages serve as a guide to the characteristics attributed to your house number.

House Number One

Positive traits: Creates good energy & positive vibrations
Negative Traits: Evokes selfishness & snobbery in negative tenants
Best Companions: Destiny Numbers 1, 3, 8

Summation: This is a trend setters dream house which calls out to be occupied by a pioneering spirit who dares take advantage of its inventive energy. This house likes plenty of sunlight and fresh air. Exotic plants, trees, and flowers are good companions, and the positive vibrations are enhanced by the colors yellow, gold and orange. A Number 1 house requires a good fire alarm system because it is subject to fire hazards.

House Number Two

Positive traits: Creates peace, harmony & balance
Negative Traits: Evokes laziness & insecurity in negative tenants
Best Companions: Destiny Numbers 2, 6, 9

Summation: Not a good choice for the ambitious, career-minded spirit. This house is far better suited to laid back, friendly people. Young lovers and long-time partners suit this house because its loving vibration prefers couples to single or multiple owners. Cream, green, white decor enhance its harmonious vibration and trees and flowers native to your area suit it very well. Creaking gates and floorboards and cracked pavements need attention.

House Number Three

Positive traits: Creates a happy sociable vibration
Negative Traits: Evokes extravagance & noisiness in negative tenants
Best Companions: Destiny Numbers 1, 3, 5

Summation: This house has creative energy and a WELCOME sign. Music lovers, actors and entrepreneurs beat a path to the door. Occupants love indoor and outdoor entertaining, so quiet neighbors beware. It is a lucky house, often of unusual design. Mauve and lilac will have a calming effect on noisy, restless tenants. Owners of a Number 3 house often overinvest, sometimes creating an odd and cluttered effect

House Number Four

Positive traits: Creates an orderly existence and a secure vibration
Negative Traits: Has an unlived appearance when occupied by negative tenants
Best Companions: Destiny Numbers 4, 7, 8

Summation: Bars on the windows, locks on the doors will be the general impression this house gives when occupied by negative tenants. It welcomes neat, orderly occupants who will keep repairs up to date. Blue, gray muted colors are favorites, and being an earthy house, it likes lots of indoor plants. Structural problems are sometimes a headache for the owners.

House Number Five

Positive traits: Creates challenges & an uninhibited vibration
Negative Traits: Evokes arguments & bad tempers in negative tenants
Best Companions: Destiny Numbers 1, 3, 5

Summation: A Number 5 house often becomes labeled "a temporary dwelling" because the vibration is one of change, challenge and new experience, thus encouraging its tenants to move on or to be frequently away from home, leaving the premises subject to break and enter. And even when they don't submit to these urges, they find themselves forever changing the decor. Variety is the key word, so the owner often has different ideas for every room. Pictures of this house seem to have a spot reserved in the estate agent's window.

House Number Six

Positive traits: Creates a peaceful, loving, tranquil vibration
Negative Traits: Evokes interference & jealousy from negative neighbors
Best Companions: Destiny Numbers 2, 3, 4, 6, 9

Summation: There are few people who are not attracted to a Number 6 house, because its loving vibration is most appealing. It evokes considerate, romantic, creative and homely instincts from its tenants. Music enhances these positive traits, and even negative tenants benefit from the harmonious forces in a 6 house. It is family orientated and an exquisite rose garden is often cultivated by its owners.

House Number Seven

Positive traits: Creates a serene, mystical vibration
Negative Traits: Evokes secretiveness & loneliness in negative tenants
Best Companions: Destiny Numbers 7, 9

Summation: Mystical, intellectual, philosophical, imaginative spirits are captured by the vibration of a 7 house, as are seekers of solitude. This house encourages its occupants to develop their spiritual and psychic abilities. Wishing wells, ponds, fountains and pools enhance its serenity. Orchids and four leaf clovers love this dwelling, but can evoke loneliness and secretiveness in negative tenants. Problems with the plumbing system often arise in a 7 house.

House Number Eight

Positive traits: Creates ambition & material benefits
Negative Traits: Evokes extreme behavioral patterns in negative tenants
Best Companions: Destiny Numbers 1, 4, 8

Summation: A Number 8 house complements the hard-working, ambitious qualities of positive tenants. People best suited to a Number 8 house are focused business types who know how to make every goal a winner. It is a solid house whose owners keep it that way. Moss green and cream, blues and grays, all suit the 8 house. Trees, plants and flowers native to the area enhance this dwelling. An extreme of behavior and character traits are common in negative tenants.

House Number Nine

Positive traits: Creates humanitarian, vocational instincts in its occupants
Negative Traits: Evokes self-righteous sanctimonious behavior in negative tenants
Best Companions: Destiny Numbers 2, 6, 9

Summation: A 9 house inspires mental and spiritual growth so will attract medical people, visionaries, welfare workers. People who create an atmosphere of belonging are welcome. Its garden loves daffodils, roses and carnations. Psychic awareness may be evoked in its occupants. This is however an accident prone environment for negative tenants.

SOME COMBINATION NUMBER EXAMPLES

Name: Imelda Keyes   **Birth Date**: 24-5-1986

I M E L D A   K E Y E S
9+4+5+3+4+1 + 2+5+7+5+1= 46   4+6=10=1   2+4+5+1+9+8+6 = 35 3+5 = 8

		PERSONALITY BOX

Destiny Number   8
Zodiac Number   5
Name Number   1
Birthpath Number   6

PERSONALITY BOX

	6	9
2	5	8
1	4	

Health	Skin problems such as eczema and psoriasis; rheumatism; intestinal problems; gall bladder; spleen problems
Lucky Colors	Dark blue; purple; gray; black
Lucky Gemstones	Rubies; dark sapphires; black diamonds
Lucky Lottery Numbers	1 — 8 — 17 — 26 — 35 — 44
Best Companions	Destiny Numbers 1 — 4 — 8
Lucky Years	1988 — 1997 — 2006 — 2015 — 2024 — 2033 — 2042 — 2051 — 2060 — 2069

PERSONALITY PROFILE

Imelda's Destiny Number 8 dictates that her karmic lessons will include a feast or famine/all or nothing lifestyle. But even though she can expect some difficult lessons, she will also experience the joy of success. Fate will expect nothing less than her best effort in achieving her goals — the "piper" demands his pound of flesh from her, having given her the strength and skills required for her journey through life (as shown by her Destiny 8/Zodiac 5 combination). She also has a well-balanced sense of judgment, a strong will, the determination and will to succeed and is capable of being a loyal spouse and wonderful parent (as shown in her Personality Box). Her Personality Box also shows that Imelda will be a loyal and honest friend, but will not suffer fools easily. As a child, Imelda will show potential for leadership; but she will be mischievous and impatient, at worst an intolerant and bossy show-off. She needs early discipline and positive encouragement or her guardians will be forever apologizing for their "rebel ringleader". As an adult she will be busy experiencing all that life has to offer. Her 8/5 combination will make her want to live life to the full, at times being reckless, at others imposing strict discipline on herself in her quest for happiness. As a mature person, Imelda will have many tales of adventure to tell her grandchildren, whom she will expect to be replicas of herself. Because of her love of life, Imelda will resent such ailments as rheumatism and bladder problems, which will make her a difficult patient in her old age. But Imelda is a battler and will not succumb easily to illness of any kind.

Name: John Black   **Birth Date**: 10-3-1963

J O H N   B L A C K
$1+6+8+5 + 2+3+1+3+2 = 31$ $3+1 = 4$ $1+0+3+1+9+6+3 = 23$ $2+3 = 5$

Destiny Number	5
Zodiac Number	7
Name Number	4
Birthpath Number	3

PERSONALITY BOX

$^3{}_3$	6	9
$^1{}_1$		

Health	Insomnia; nervous disorders; over active thyroid; respiratory problems
Lucky Colors	Gray and other light colors
Lucky Gemstones	Diamonds
Lucky Lottery Numbers	4 — 5 — 14 — 23 — 32 — 41
Best Companions	Destiny Numbers 1 — 3 — 8
Lucky Years	1967 — 1976 — 1985 — 1994 — 2003 — 2012 — 2021 — 2030 — 2039 — 2048

PERSONALITY PROFILE

Travel, change, challenge and new experiences are the key words for John's destiny. Fate has dealt him a wide variety of karmic lessons with which to fulfill his commitment to life. He no doubt views his life as though looking through a kaleidoscope — blink your eye and the pattern has changed. As if to make things more interesting — or annoying — John's inclination will be to find solitude. Fate will often deny him the privacy he craves to explore his extremely intelligent, creative and philosophical mind (as shown in his Personality Box). His wish to pay serious attention to his scholastic and creative studies will be all too often distracted by fated intervention when his karmic destiny decrees he should be involved — albeit temporarily — in more earthly pursuits. His awkward Destiny 5/Zodiac 7 combination inclines him to clumsiness, sometimes resulting in minor, annoying accidents. As a child, John would have seemed inclined to hang back at school, not wishing to enjoy the limelight — a wasted effort — because his teachers would not have failed to see the intellectual talent of this student. As an adult, he is likely to be using his innate desire to travel to remote places, where he can further develop his creative/philosophical skills. His reputation for being a focused, loyal, hard-worker (Name Number 4) will be well rewarded by his employers and appreciated by his spouse and children. Insomnia may well be a problem for John because the privacy and solitude he so often seeks may only be gained when everyone else is asleep. The inevitable hectic pattern of his Number 5 karmic destiny is necessary to his commitment to this incarnation.

Name: Jim Newman **Birth Date:** 14-8-1974

J I M N E W M A N
1+9+4 + 5+5+5+4+1+5 = 39 3+9 = 12 1+2=3   1+4+8+1+9+7+4 = 34 3+4 = 7

Destiny Number	7	
Zodiac Number	1	
Name Number	3	
Birthpath Number	5	

PERSONALITY BOX

		9
		8
1 1	4 4	7

Health	Spinal problems; bladder problems; mood swings
Lucky Colors	Yellow; gold; green
Lucky Gemstones	Moonstone; agate
Lucky Lottery Numbers	3 — 7 — 16 — 25 — 34 — 43
Best Companions	Destiny Numbers 2 — 4 — 6
Lucky Years	1978 — 1987 — 1996 — 2005 — 2014 — 2023 — 2032 — 2041 — 2050 — 2059

PERSONALITY PROFILE

There will be no stopping the growth and expansion, pioneering, creative and physical energy flow (shown in Jim's Personality Box and combined 1–3–5 major number influences) from plaguing the karmically-inspired solitary and serene lifestyle Jim's commitment to his destiny compels him to follow. In this incarnation, Jim must become "the Searcher" for a higher understanding of how best to combine raw physical energy with philosophical, imaginative, intellectual power for the benefit and progress of his inner spirit. His Personality Box shows how the physically active side of his nature will inevitably bring friends and admirers flocking around him to observe his many and unique talents; but the power of his Number 7 Destiny path will make him hard to find, then resentful of this intrusion, causing envy and misunderstanding from his friends and family. As a child he was one step ahead of his peers, though his reserved nature ensured modesty. As an adult, he is the elusive charmer, probably and rightly earning him the title "Gentleman Jim". The fear of marital commitment will make him a perpetual bachelor who will not mind becoming a lonely old man. Jim can never be lonely in his own company, there are too many intellectual adventures to keep him happy. Apart from the occasional bladder problem, Jim will cope well enough with other minor irritations that old age may bring. If he seems to "step lively" and yet be aloof, it will be because he is walking to a different tune to the majority, for Jim will refuse to ignore his inner voice.

Name: Betty Brown   **Birth Date:** 21-12-1933

BETTY BROWN
2+5+2+2+7 + 2+9+6+5+5 = 45   4+5 = 9   2+1+1+2+1+9+3+3 = 22   2+2 = 4

Destiny Number	4
Zodiac Number	3
Name Number	9
Birthpath Number	3

PERSONALITY BOX

3_3		9
2_2		
1_1		

Health	Neck and head problems; bouts of cramp; anemia
Lucky Colors	Lilac; mauve; violet
Lucky Gemstones	Amethyst; garnet
Lucky Lottery Numbers	4 — 9 — 13 — 22 — 31 — 40
Best Companions	Destiny Numbers 1 — 4 — 8
Lucky Years	1939 — 1948 — 1957 — 1966 — 1975 — 1984 — 1993 — 2002 — 2011 — 2020

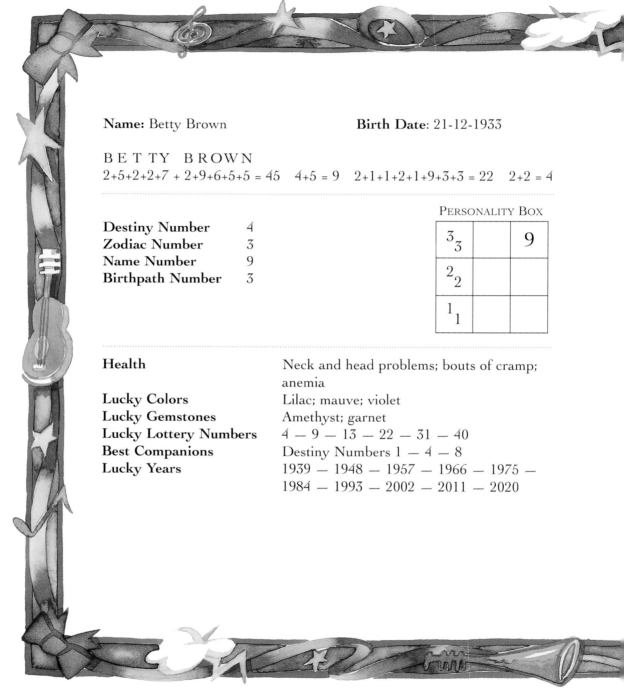

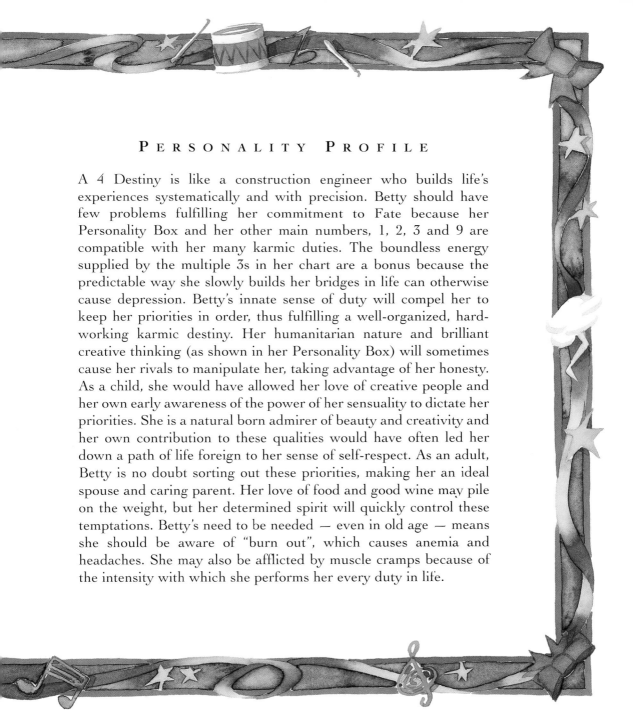

PERSONALITY PROFILE

A 4 Destiny is like a construction engineer who builds life's experiences systematically and with precision. Betty should have few problems fulfilling her commitment to Fate because her Personality Box and her other main numbers, 1, 2, 3 and 9 are compatible with her many karmic duties. The boundless energy supplied by the multiple 3s in her chart are a bonus because the predictable way she slowly builds her bridges in life can otherwise cause depression. Betty's innate sense of duty will compel her to keep her priorities in order, thus fulfilling a well-organized, hard-working karmic destiny. Her humanitarian nature and brilliant creative thinking (as shown in her Personality Box) will sometimes cause her rivals to manipulate her, taking advantage of her honesty. As a child, she would have allowed her love of creative people and her own early awareness of the power of her sensuality to dictate her priorities. She is a natural born admirer of beauty and creativity and her own contribution to these qualities would have often led her down a path of life foreign to her sense of self-respect. As an adult, Betty is no doubt sorting out these priorities, making her an ideal spouse and caring parent. Her love of food and good wine may pile on the weight, but her determined spirit will quickly control these temptations. Betty's need to be needed — even in old age — means she should be aware of "burn out", which causes anemia and headaches. She may also be afflicted by muscle cramps because of the intensity with which she performs her every duty in life.

CONCLUSION

You now have a numerology manual at your disposal, complete with all the relevant information you will need to assess your personality and forecast your future. The information you gain from this manual is invaluable in fulfilling the possibilities and probabilities in your destiny.

When making choices in life, imagine the benefit if you were aware of possible, even likely pitfalls, and were ready for the opportunities which come your way. Timing is all important to achievement in life; so if you know what time you should be in what place, you are at an immediate advantage. Numerology can enlighten you to these facts.

Any insight you gain into a child's personality is beneficial to all concerned. Misunderstood children become dysfunctional adults, and they and all who know them suffer for this mistake.

Adults who understand their inner selves and the forces to which they are susceptible can make the most of what life offers them. Those who take the time to understand their companions and forces within their society reap just reward.

Learning the secrets of the Personality Box is well worth the effort. The advantages which the information in these magic boxes within a box will yield is worth knowing.

Numerology is a fascinating subject and one which will supply you with as much entertainment as insight. It is natural to be curious about your own and other people's personalities, and you will soon gain the reputation for having sound judgment.

Understanding is the key word to peace of mind and personal happiness. This you can achieve with the assistance of the art of numerology.

NOTES

For Sam and Kimberley

This edition published by Barnes & Noble, Inc., by arrangment with
Lansdowne Publishing.

1998 Barnes & Noble Books
M 10 9 8 7 6 5 4 3
ISBN 0- 7607-0932-7

Published by Lansdowne Publishing Pty Ltd
Level 1, 18 Argyle Street, Sydney NSW 2000, Australia

First published 1997
Reprinted in 1998, 1999

© Copyright text, illustration and design:
Lansdowne Publishing Pty Ltd 1996

Designer: Sylvie Abecassis
Editor: Cynthia Blanche
Illustrators: Penny Lovelock, Sue Ninham

Set in Cochin and Bauer Text Initials on QuarkXpress
Printed in Singapore by Tien Wah Press Pte Ltd